T0132399

Layla Loves Cookies

LaTanya Ward-Showers

Illustrated by Gabriela Altamirano

AuthorHouse™
1663 Liberty Drive
Bloomington, IN 47403
www.authorhouse.com
Phone: 1 (800) 839-8640

Published by AuthorHouse: 09/04/2015

ISBN: 978-1-5049-3129-8 (sc)
ISBN: 978-1-5049-3130-4 (e)

Print information available on the last page.

Any people depicted in stock imagery provided by Thinkstock are models,
and such images are being used for illustrative purposes only.
Certain stock imagery © Thinkstock.

This book is printed on acid-free paper.

authorHOUSE®

SUGAR, TRIPLE CHOCOLATE, PEANUT BUTTER, and COCONUT are some of Layla's FAVORITE cookies!!

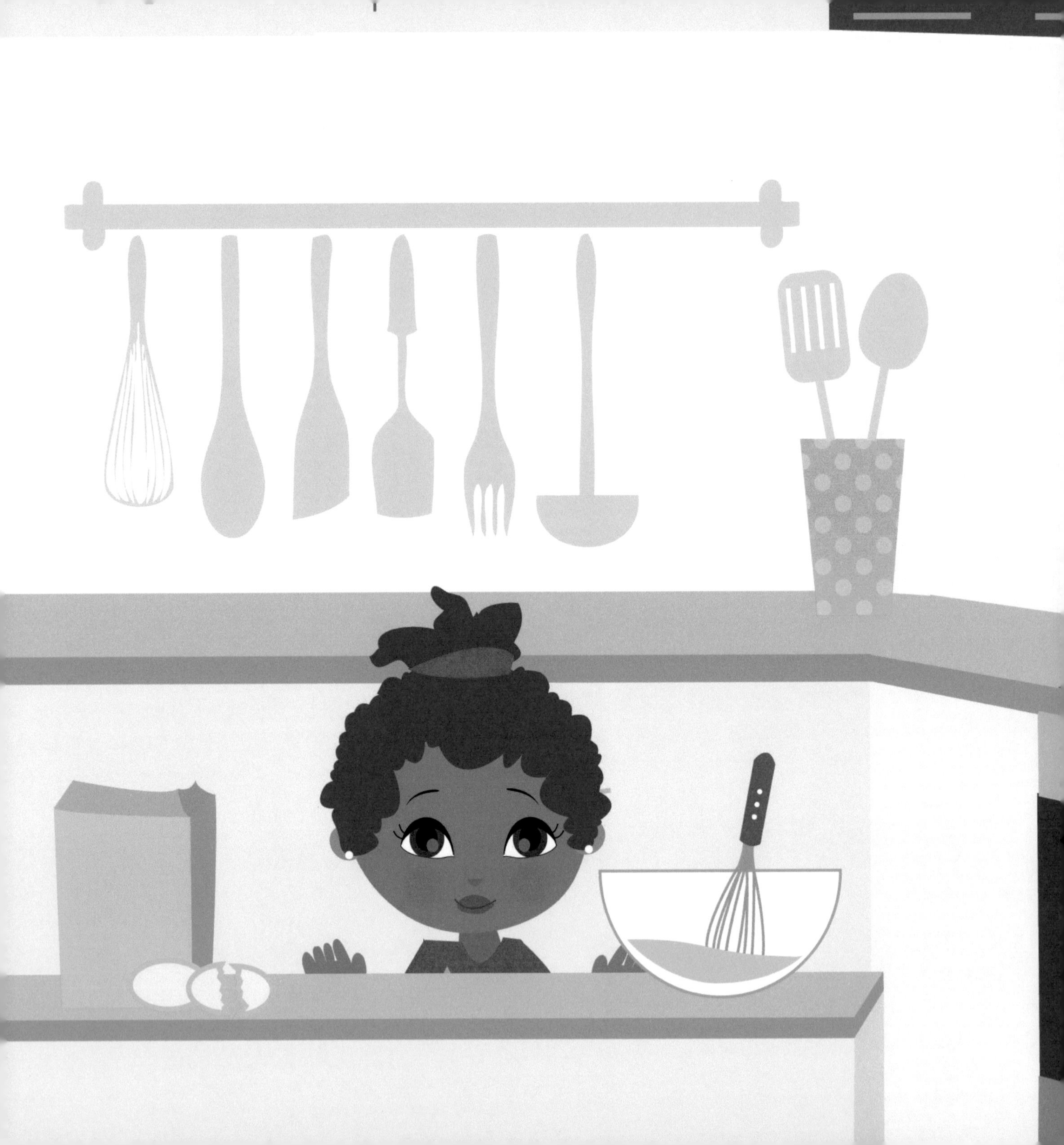

It is easy to get Layla in the kitchen when cookies are involved! Licking the spoon, waiting patiently by the oven, and the yummy smell makes it a challenge to keep Layla away until the cookies cool down. Warm cookies are just minutes out of the oven now and Layla can hardly wait for her first bite!

Tasty cookies are Layla's preferred snack and she could eat them all day, but her parents limit her to just two cookies for an after dinner snack. She doesn't like this rule, so she decides she will sneak some cookies out of the cookie jar in the kitchen once everyone is asleep. And she hopes her parents do not catch her.

3

Layla's bedroom is right next to the kitchen so she plans to quietly run in for the cookies and then hurry back to bed to begin her snack! All sounds like an easy plan except for one thing; Layla shares a bedroom with her big sister Hannah. And if her sister catches her she is sure to tattle.

Layla wonders how she will be able to sneak the cookies by her sister without getting caught. "For the love of cookies I'll put a plan to the test!" exclaims Layla.

The first night while everyone is sleeping Layla quietly runs to the kitchen and is able to sneak a few cookies. But, turns out Layla was not sneaky enough because Hannah is sitting straight up in bed when Layla makes it back to the bedroom. "What are you doing out of bed?" Hannah asks. Layla is in shock so she doesn't answer her sister right away. Hannah proceeds as if she is going to yell and tattle to their parents so Layla hurries and gives her a cookie so she will keep quiet. Hannah still has an untrusting look on her face so in order to stay out of trouble Layla agrees to give her two cookies and she keeps just one for herself. "Looks like they are my cookies now," says Hannah as she takes the two cookies from Layla.

Neither mommy nor daddy have noticed there are cookies missing from the cookie jar so on the second night Layla intends to try again except for a small change to her original plans. She did not like having to share her cookies with her big sister so she decided she would wait until Hannah was in a deep sleep before sneaking to the kitchen. Hannah was finally in bed snoring away so Layla quietly heads to the kitchen. This time she makes it to the kitchen and back to bed with the cookies!

Everything seems to have worked out well except that Layla was so caught up in how delicious the cookies were she did not realize she was smacking! Layla is enjoying her cookies thinking she is in the clear until Hannah wakes up from all the loud smacking noise.

Hannah was wary in her glance at Layla and not at all happy about having her sleep interrupted. Again, Hannah is about to yell and tattle so Layla gives her the last cookie to keep her quiet. "Not my last cookie," cries Layla as she returns to bed disappointed about her failed plan.

Layla doesn't realize that after the second night Hannah is not the only person she has to worry about. Unbeknownst to Layla her parents have noticed the low amount of cookies in the cookie jar. Parents really notice everything and they will research any suspicious activity until they get to the bottom of it. But, will they figure out Layla is the cookie snatcher?

Even with the two letdowns, Layla is determined to sneak cookies all for herself. Yes, believe it or not, even with her past defeat Layla is going to try a different plan. The third night is approaching and Layla's main focus is not surrendering any of her hard earned cookies to her big sister.

Since she wants all the cookies to herself she decides she will not sneak the cookies into the bedroom where Hannah is sure to wake up. Instead, she will sit quietly and eat the cookies in the dark kitchen. Layla decides if her sister catches her out of bed she will tell her that she was up to get a drink of water.

Layla makes it to the kitchen, sneaks a few cookies, and begins to enjoy the tasty cookies in the dark kitchen. "Finally, cookie snatching success!" exclaims Layla. As she is into her first bite she hears a "click" noise and the kitchen light comes on! "Oh no it's daddy," cries Layla. "So you're the cookie snatcher," says Layla's dad. Embarrassed and with no good excuse Layla apologizes and is sent off to bed.

21

Layla continues to receive cookies as a snack after her dinner, but no more sneaking cookies! Once it is bedtime; SUGAR, TRIPLE CHOCOLATE, PEANUT BUTTER, and COCONUT are only in her dreams and definitely not in the bed!

LaTanya Ward-Showers is an author of children's fiction literature that exposes children to empowered lead characters of color. "I remember growing up loving short stories and always wondered why I never saw characters that looked like me."

As early as the third grade LaTanya began writing short stories with the encouragement of her teacher and parents. Her passion for multicultural literature grew further when she became a mother.

In 2013 LaTanya released her first children's book Could It Be A Monster In The Attic?. It's an enjoyable tale about capturing a monster in the attic with a surprising twist at the end. The story is dedicated to her young son. "If my short stories never make it into any other home, I at least want to do this for my son." Thankfully her stories have made it into the hands of many children. Her latest title Layla is a series centered on an adventurous young girl who is powerful and goal oriented. Since her first publication, LaTanya has received reviews and feedback from other parents and educators thanking her for creating stories with positive storylines. They have been elated because she's encouraging multicultural literature. Other recognitions include appearances at schools and libraries for inspirational speaking and spotlight artist for different publications.

LaTanya received a B.A. in Psychology from the University of Texas at San Antonio and lives in Texas with her husband and young son. Her approach to writing children's books is to keep it simple with everyday fun stories while leaving room for the imagination to stretch. Much of her writing draws on her childhood experiences and she also credits her son for inspiring her through his enthusiasm for life.

LaTanya divides her time up between writing and style contributions for plus size fashion.

Printed in the United States
by Baker & Taylor Publisher Services